To the breeders who made today's guppies possible.

Endpapers: This tankful of mixed male guppies presents an image of color and action—two of the prime ingredients in the recipe for aquarium enjoyment.

A Beginner's Guide To
Guppies

Written By
Carroll Friswold

Contents

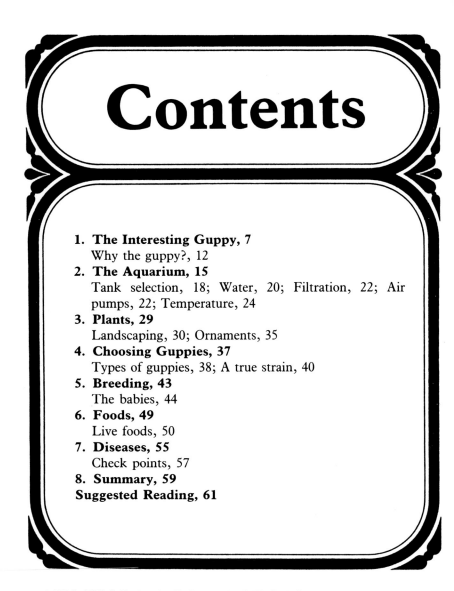

JUN 12 1994

1.
The interesting guppy

When you decided to get some guppies, I think you made a very good choice, one that you will find enjoyable. They are one of the most interesting of all the fishes that we keep in our aquaria, so let's talk a little about them.

This "mixed bag" of fancy guppies very nicely accents the beauty of a water lily.

Mature male variegated fantail guppies. The specialized intromittent organ, the gonopodium, is visible on several individuals here; the fin develops early, making it possible to sex guppies several weeks before they reach maturity.

The guppy in its natural habitat. These wild fish, photographed in a mangrove swamp, are well camouflaged from predators and are a far cry from the brightly colored fancy guppy strains available to the hobbyist and breeder today.

First of all, the guppy is a small fish, from 1 to 2 inches in length, native to the northern sections of South America and some of the islands of the Caribbean and living in such numbers as to be called the "millions" fish. In nature it is usually of a dull greenish gray color, sometimes with faint green, red, or blue markings, and with short fins and tail—altogether different from the tame strains with their beautiful, sometimes even gorgeous, colors in numberless patterns, designs, and combinations, with tails and fins in all sorts of variations, long, short, wide, etc.

It is a viviparous species, that is, the young are born alive. Most other fishes lay eggs. The male has his anal fin modified into a gonopodium, a special arrangement of the fin rays that allows him to introduce a sperm packet into the female during mating. Because the gonopodium is recognizable very early, it is possible to sex guppies several weeks before they mature.

History

The guppy was first scientifically examined and named by the German scientist Wilhelm Peters in 1859, using specimens from a shipment of fishes collected in Venezuela. He called it *Poecilia reticulata*. However, after various studies and reclassifications, the fish was put into the genus *Lebistes* by Dr. C.T. Regan in 1913, becoming *Lebistes reticulatus*. The name *Lebistes reticulatus* stuck with our guppy all through its growth in popularity as an aquarium fish. However, in 1963 the American ichthyologists Doctors Rosen and Bailey showed that the name first given to the guppy was the correct one, *Poecilia reticulata*.

Some guppy strains display a delicate array of pastel hues that offer a nice contrast to the more strongly colored and patterned black and red delta-type fish.

The popular name "guppy" was given to the little fish in honor of one Rev. Dr. R.J. Lechemere Guppy, who in 1866 sent some specimens to the British Museum for identification. It came about through popular usage rather than Rev. Dr. Guppy's having anything to do with the choice of name.

Why the guppy?

The guppy has many fine qualities. It is hardy, both as to climate and living conditions. It is not shy and does not continually hide as so many of the other fishes do; it will most likely be right out in the middle of the tank flirting and showing off. The guppy is a good community tank fish, although it will do best with its own kind. It is usually a sure breeder. It is not fussy about food, readily accepting either dry or live foods. The guppy is not a fighter. Guppies mature rapidly, a characteristic that is of great advantage to the breeder who is trying to bring out and fix certain colors or other variations. Altogether, the guppy is probably the most satisfactory of all aquarium fishes.

The degree and variety of finnage can vary considerably among fancy guppies, even among those of the same basic strain. These are both black delta-type fish, but the upper fish is a flagtail with a shorter dorsal fin, while the lower specimen is a square flagtail with the much longer dorsal sought by breeders. Photo by Andre Roth.

2.
The aquarium

Before discussing how to choose your guppies, let's give a bit of thought to the world in which they are to live. An aquarium is a little world of its own, separate from

Facing page: *Black delta flagtails. The "half-black" fancy guppies were among the first developed and are still enormously popular with hobbyists. Photo by Andre Roth.* **Above:** *A unique and beautiful home aquarium unit designed and built by Werner Pacagnella of Bologna, Italy.*

The highly popular snakesin guppies come in a near-infinite variety of patterns, with nearly as much variation as can be found in the human fingerprint. This is a yellow snakesin fantail. Photo by R. Zukal.

its room surroundings as to temperature and water conditions. Generally in use is the rectangular, all-glass aquarium. You will also find a reflector and hood with electrical fittings for lighting the aquarium to be most useful, as it will keep fish in and other things out of the tank. Many people prefer fluorescent fittings and the long-lived and low-heat tubes. In the use of fluorescent equipment, do not use the blue or white tubes—use those having the word "warm," such as warm white, warm tint, warm tone. Tubes are available that give off a large amount of the red rays in their spectrums; these accent or rather intensify the colors of the fish, especially the red and orange shades. Also, as they were developed for greenhouse use, they help the growth of your plants. If your present reflector is fitted for regular incandescent light bulbs and you wish to change to fluorescent with its low-heat and long-life tubes, adapters may be purchased and easily installed, and these are quite effective.

Tank selection

In choosing a tank several points should be taken into consideration. Never pick a tank on price alone; inferior materials and poor workmanship can never give satisfaction and are sure to cause trouble, which usually comes at the most awkward time when no help is available. Choose an aquarium with a well-glued frame and without gobs of extra cement. Examine the glass in the aquarium carefully to make sure it can hold the water volume you have in mind. In a small tank, say of 5 gallons capacity or less, you can get by with using single strength glass; tanks of larger capacity must have thicker glass. Check especially the bottom for sufficient thickness and strength. Water weighs 8⅓ pounds per

Careful selection of the tank, accessories, and decorations will go a long way toward avoiding dissatisfaction and disappointment in the future. Never choose a new tank based on price alone; better to invest a bit more at the beginning than to have big problems with an inferior product later on! Photo by Dr. Herbert R. Axelrod.

gallon, so that means a 5-gallon tank holds about 43 pounds, while a 15-gallon tank has to hold 125 pounds of water alone—all of these things must be considered. Also of importance, the tank must be located so as to be level and even; if this is neglected you will soon have trouble, as the cement seal will loosen and the water leak out. Be careful in setting it up. Bottoms of larger tanks may be made of heavier glass or even of slate.

Beware of tanks with thin glass and irregular gluing—these cannot possibly give you satisfactory service. I keep emphasizing this because it is very important. Before making a final choice, compare tanks and you will begin to notice these differences.

Also, if you have a choice between two sizes of tanks of equal quality and you have the space to accommodate either, *always choose the larger*—you will be glad you did as it is easier to care for and you will get better results from your fish.

Your guppies will do so much better if they have enough room to swim around and stretch a little. Sure, guppies can be raised in a bowl or a glass jar, but the fine ones are not raised that way. The fine ones come from aquaria with a good amount of room, proper heat and light, good food, and clean, clear water. Of course, you have to have good quality stock with which to work—this we will discuss as we go along.

Water

Next let us consider the water in which your guppies are to live. Actually, water is a tremendously complex subject, and every part of the country, and for that matter,

20

A pair of multicolor delta fantails, showing the popular "leopard," or "zebra," tail pattern. These two individuals display a similar "wild-type" color pattern on the body but vary considerably in the shape and pattern of the dorsal and caudal fins. Photo by H. Kyselov.

the world, has water different from every other region. It contains all sorts of minerals and buffers, in millions of combinations in solutions of varying strengths. The guppy has a wide range of tolerance, living in soft or acid water, but it prefers clean, clear water at 78°F. Use your local water, and if the fish do not prosper, you can begin to change the chemical content to make it more comfortable. This can be done by simply gradually adding distilled water if you wish to cut down the mineral content or by adding peat water to soften the water and add certain minerals. Remember that any changes should be made very gradually—do not just dump a lot of chemicals into the tank and let it go at that.

Filtration

One of the greatest helps in keeping the water clean and clear is a good filtering system in which the tank water is run through filter floss or another filter bed, then through charcoal granules, and then back into the tank by means of an air lift, which requires an air pump to make it go. Filters may be of various types, including undergravel filters, corner filters, and those most commonly in use that hang from the frame outside the tank, usually on the back. Talk it over with the people at your pet shop and they will help you select the filter best suited for your setup.

Air pumps

Filters require air pumps to furnish the stream of air required to lift the "cleaned" water back into the aquarium. Even if a power filter (which uses a water pump to move the water) is used, an air pump is usually needed

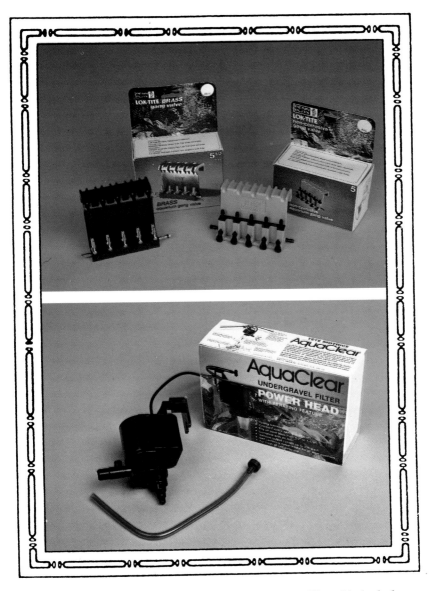

There are many fine products on the market that will enable both the beginning and the advanced hobbyist to maintain and breed guppies with a minimum of problems. Photos by Vince Serbin.

to help aerate the water. Here again consult your dealer because not all pumps are of equal quality or of equal capacity and they come in all sorts of prices. There are piston pumps and vibrator-diaphragm types, and for large installations there are the compressor types with their low pressure and great volume.

Your filter should be run at such a rate that a considerable volume of water goes through it per hour, yet you do not want it to be blasting so the tank is in a continual turmoil. Also, change the filtering material whenever it is too full of dirt to do a proper job, and rinse the charcoal each time you change the floss. To obtain the correct volume of air in your filter you may wish to cut down the big airstream, which is easily done by inserting a 3-way valve into your air line and then opening the valve till you have the exact amount you wish to use, the excess air simply blowing into the room. It is also wise to have a filter outfit for each separate tank; then if disease should break out (and it can at any time) it is not carried to other tanks. One pump may be used to run several filters.

Temperature

Temperature is important in the life of the guppy. Somewhere between 75 and 80°F—is perfect. Females carrying young are especially sensitive to becoming chilled—a great many females die from chill, especially in the spring and fall when temperatures can drop rather suddenly. If they do not die they can pick up "ich" or fungus.

Although the hardy and adaptable guppy is reasonably resistant to changes in temperature, control of the temperature level is most important at all times, especially in the case of females carrying young. Invest in a reliable heater and an accurate thermometer to be on the safe side. Photo by Dr. Herbert R. Axelrod.

To forestall any troubles caused by chilling, just put a heater and thermostat into the tank. Usually this is a glass tube with a resistance unit or coil that is activated by the action of a bimetallic strip within a predetermined range; say that it begins heating at 75°F and shuts off when the water reaches 80°F. Many heater-thermostats are easily adjustable by the turning of a button. Of course, the above is for the individual tank; in a large setup or a room with many aquaria you would probably heat the whole room.

It is good insurance to have a heater in the guppy tank—if warmth is required the thermostat makes connection and turns on the heater; if heat is not needed, the thermostat just sits there and the fish are still protected.

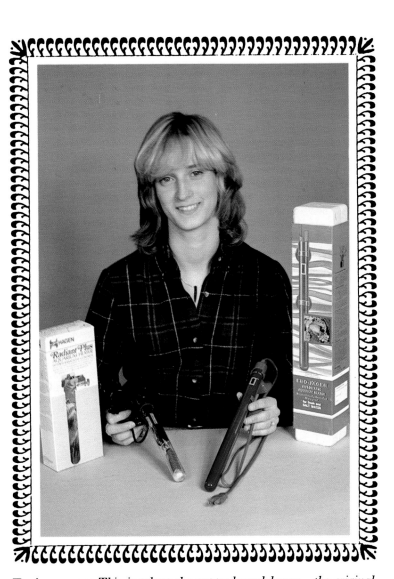

Facing page: *This is where the guppy legend began—the original wild guppy from Trinidad and northern South America. As can be seen from this photo, the original guppy was nothing to really rave about, and vast improvements have been made through the efforts of breeders.* **Above:** *Don't skimp in the choice of a tank heater—a bad choice or the purchase of an inferior unit could cost you dearly in lost fish later on! Photo by Dr. Herbert R. Axelrod.*

3.
Plants

Aquatic plants are very interesting in themselves and can be a great attraction in the tank as well as valuable for the oxygen they generate and release into the water

Facing page: *The venerable half-black red delta of the aquarium trade. In spite of the great variety of fancy guppies available to the aquarist today, this attractive strain remains high on the popularity list. Photo by Dr. Harry Grier.* **Above:** *Nothing completes the total aquarium picture more effectively and beautifully than the presence of living plants.*

and for the carbon dioxide and fish droppings they absorb.

Plants may be of either the rooted or the floating type—one or a combination of both will be equally satisfactory. Rooted plants may be planted in the gravel of the tank or in separate ceramic containers that sit on top of the gravel or may be dug down into the gravel. Gravels may be obtained either in natural colors or artificially colored in many sizes and materials.

The usual purpose of the floating plants is to give some protection and act as a hiding place for the newborn babies. There are many excellent floating plants: *Najas*, *Riccia*, hornwort, the bladderworts, *Nitella*, watersprite, etc. Rooted plants are also of great value, with the *Sagittaria* species at the head of the list, both as to their great variety and availability and for the work they do. Another group of very great value is the genus *Cryptocoryne*. These are Orientals and come in many sizes, colors, and shapes of leaves. Several species will even bloom in the aquarium; for instance, the flower of *Cryptocoryne griffithii* is a beautiful dark red and looks like a small lily. All are excellent producers of oxygen. Another valuable trait of the Cryptocorynes is that they require less light to prosper than almost any other aquarium plants; they usually grow beautifully in dim or diffused light, giving off oxygen at the point where other plants quit and begin absorbing oxygen from the water in the tank.

Landscaping

Plants also have another desirable feature: they beautify the aquarium. You will find landscaping the aquarium

Tank ornaments may vary all the way from natural rocks and wood to the many novelty ornaments available in pet shops. Choose ornaments carefully so as to avoid those that may allow wastes and debris to accumulate unseen. Photo by Dr. D. Terver, Nancy Aquarium, France.

A guppy display tank is the scene of constant activity as the energetic little fish, even though hampered by their luxuriant tails, dart about in the search for food. These are blue snakeskin fantails.

The brightly colored male is beginning to make his courtship display to the female.

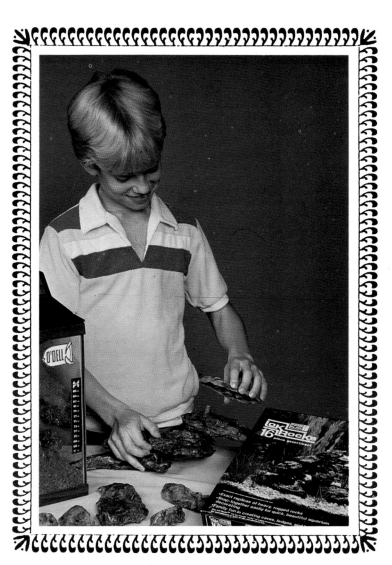

There are many artificial rock and cave kits available today that take much of the risk out of using natural rocks as decorations in the aquarium. Even artificial rockwork should be set up to minimize crevices where wastes may accumulate. Photo by Dr. Herbert R. Axelrod.

is very interesting and rewarding; there are no set rules as to planting—you are the one who has to live with it, so fix it up to suit your own taste. There is no limit to the possible variations as to the plants used, their leaf shapes, the color shadings of the tints of green, red, bronze, etc. For instance, at some large shows an aquarium at one time would not even be considered in competition unless there was at least three distinct shades of green in the plants!

Plants come in dozens of shades of green and in many sizes and shapes and textures of leaves, running from the simple grass-like blade through long, short, thick, thin, narrow, wide, round, to the fabulous Madagascar laceleaf with its intricate tracery and openings like a piece of green embroidery.

Plants will usually prosper with a minimum six to eight hours of light per day; this can vary with types of plants used, location of aquarium in the room, and the season of the year.

Ornaments

Plants may be used by themselves or in combination with other materials such as glassware, ceramics, or rocks. Metals usually are not considered good aquarium materials, but safe rocks come in every possible color, texture, shape, and size. Agates, jaspers, obsidians, and granites are all good, and petrified wood comes in all colors and grains. You can really dress up your aquarium with special rocks for backgrounds, even using complementary colors for your colored fish. Beware of, or at least take a very careful look at, all green or blue rocks. Many are harmless, but some might just possibly contain copper or arsenic, both of which are deadly to fishes and plants.

4.
Choosing guppies

Now, let's discuss what will probably be your most important decision, the choice of your fish. Oh sure, you can go into the shop and ask for a pair of guppies, and that is all you will get, just two small fish of no distinc-

Facing page: Red and yellow make one of the most pleasing color combinations in guppies, as this beautiful male shows. Photo by H. J. Richter. **Above:** *Note the contrast between the male and female fancy guppies shown in this group of variegated snakeskin deltas. Photo by H. Kiselov.*

tion at all. On the other hand, with a bit of thought and effort, you can get fish you will enjoy working with and your returns will be so much more fun. Guppies come in all sorts of colors and combinations, in many varieties of fins and tails. Often there is considerable variation in a litter with the same father and mother. These variations, plus their changes and developments, are transmitted from one generation to the next, and certain of these changes are used by the fancier to develop the kind of guppy he prefers. For instance, you can have a fish you like of a certain color or with a long dorsal fin or a wide tail—any of these characteristics can be transmitted and intensified by careful selection, and in this way fine strains of guppies may be built up. The word "strain" in this connection is used to indicate what might be called a family group of guppies, related to each other and showing certain characteristics in greater or lesser degree, but all carrying the inheritance factors of that family. These factors are called genes.

Types of guppies

By now you probably have some ideas of what sort of guppy you would like to have in your aquarium—the main colors are red, blue, green and variegated; personally, I prefer a clear bright color, but many people like delicate or pastel shades. Tails come in many variations, from the very wide full delta shape to the long, thin ribbon tail, as well as upper and lower single swords, plus the double sword and the lyretail. There are also the round tail and the square tail. Dorsals may be long, round, or pointed, and the pectorals may be clear or color-spotted. Each of the variations is transmitted by the gene governing its development which gives you a chance to make additional varieties by combining those

This duo of variegated snakeskin fantails live up to their common name— the upper fish shows considerably more pattern on the body than the lower individual, which displays an almost clear white body. Photo by Dr. Herbert R. Axelrod.

variations you like or to refine and intensify what your fish already shows. Many good breeders believe that the male governs the color, fins, and tail while the female has more to do with conformation and size; this has not been proven but it is something to think about. It is also of great value if you can obtain a female of the same strain as the male you plan to use—this will save you a great deal of time and work.

A true strain

Quite often you can obtain guppies from some individual who is breeding them. This is a great advantage because you can then benefit from all the work that has already been done on that particular strain—if you know your breeder or dealer. Unfortunately, some dealers and breeders have the unhappy practice of selling pairs of what are represented to be good guppies. Later you find that the female, while she might be large and beautiful to look at, is not related to the male, so much time and money have been wasted as the resulting babies usually turn out to be just junk.

Be very, very careful not to buy fish from a tank in which fish are dead or dying—you could bring a deadly sickness into your own tank that could wipe out your fish.

Facing page: *A multicolored fantail guppy. This stunning fish is a female and shows much more color in the dorsal and caudal fins than most female guppies do. This is the result of patient and skillful selective breeding, and we can expect more and more variation and bright color among the females of future strains as guppy breeders work to perfect their art. Photo by Dr. Harry Grier.*

5.
Breeding

In setting up a strain of guppies, my own best results have come from what is known as linebreeding. Here is how it works. Choose a young male, big and strong, with as many of the special characteristics you like as

Facing page: A prime pair of yellow delta fantails. The female (upper fish) shows a dark gravid spot, which indicates that she is carrying young that are close to birth. Photo by H. J. Richter. **Above:** *A variegated fantail male. This fish displays a robust body and well-formed tail, the result of careful linebreeding. Photo by Hilmar Hansen, Aquarium Berlin.*

possible. The female should be of the same strain, either showing color in the tail or fins or she may be all clear. From the resulting litter choose one or two of the best young females and mate them with the original male, their father. From their first litter again pick the best female and mate her with the grandfather. By this method you will be concentrating the desired characteristics of the male, and after three to five generations you should begin to have very good fish. Should you lose your male (the longest I have kept a fine male is about three years), the only thing you can do is to pick out his best son and go on from there as before. However, if you are working with fish that have weaknesses, this concentration of blood will also intensify the weaknesses, so that in the long run you will very likely lose the whole group. If you start with good fish with no serious inherent defects, inbreeding and linebreeding will not cause trouble. Prof. Winge, of the University of Denmark, kept accurate records of a family of guppies, always using the same strain and never adding any new blood. After 24 years and a great number of generations, the final fish were larger and stronger than the original pair, so inbreeding by itself did no damage.

The babies

The first babies should arrive about four weeks after you put the pair together, and further litters should arrive at regular intervals. The female guppy is usually carrying four litters due to a delayed fertilization process and can have her litters at regular intervals even if the male has not been in the tank for some weeks or even months. Usually the babies are separated from the parents, but often the parents, if well fed, will not harm the young if they are left together. In this respect different strains act in different ways; some are real cannibals

A guppy birth in progress. A newly emerged fry can be seen near its mother's head while a second is being born. Guppies cannot be trusted with their own young, so parents should be removed from the breeding tank as soon as possible in order to ensure a high rate of fry survival. Photo by Rudolf Zukal.

45

Above: *This mother guppy is eyeing her newborn fry with something other than parental concern—she is interested in making a meal of it.* **Facing page:** *A baby guppy entering the world tail first. Shortly after birth—almost immediately, in fact—guppy fry are capable of fending for themselves without parental assistance. Photo by H. J. Richter.*

and hunt down their own young. If separated, the babies may be watched more closely and more carefully fed, with benefit to all. Feed them several times per day in tiny amounts using newly hatched brine shrimp, either fresh or frozen, and taking extra care that you do not overfeed and cause pollution of their tank. In the baby tank use snails for scavengers. Do not use normal filters here as the babies have a tendency to get into the siphon and you can lose them. Sponge filters may work safely, however. Use an airstone with a gentle stream of bubbles for circulation in the baby tank.

6.
Foods

Here is one of the absolute essentials: proper food properly fed can be of the utmost importance, while poor food can wreck your entire project, all other factors being equal. The guppy prefers a varied diet, although it

Facing page: *A variegated fantail showing a pronounced "leopard" tail pattern. This fish displays an attractive and symmetrical dorsal fin, although the tail is a bit on the ragged side.* **Above:** *Care should be exercised in the choice of prepared foods in the diet for show guppies— it should be of high protein content and should contain a good percentage of vegetable matter. Photo by Vince Serbin.*

takes either live or dry foods. Be careful in your choice of a dry food; it should be of high protein content and should contain a good percentage of vegetable matter. Dried ground shrimp meat is eagerly taken, especially as a little treat between the regular feedings. Feed your fish two or four times per day, just a small portion each time that they can clean up in five or six minutes. One big, heavy feeding per day will damage the shape of your fish and they will not do as well as on the smaller ones. The guppy has a comparatively small mouth, so do not use a coarse food—my own experience suggests that dry food passing through a 30-mesh screen is about right, but be sure to first remove the dust-size particles.

Live foods

One of the favorite foods of all guppies, old or young, large or small, is baby brine shrimp, which may be freshly hatched or frozen. Guppies will inhale brine shrimp and enjoy it even when they are full of other foods. Other live foods that are quite favorable are small daphnia, small mosquito wigglers, and on occasion small amounts of tubifex worms (these may have to be cut up if they are of the larger species). Do not feed tubifex in large amounts or keep guppies on a steady diet of worms. They are quite fattening and have a tendency to cause extra large pot-bellies, even to the point where dropsy occurs and the fish die. Small daphnia are good but may be hard to obtain. Small mosquito larvae make a marvelous food; rafts of mosquito eggs can be dropped in the aquarium and the fish will take them apart or leave them until they hatch and then relish the tiny new wigglers. Baby guppies can take more of the cut-up tubifex in proportion to the grown-ups and usually grow very well on it. Microworms are an excellent food and

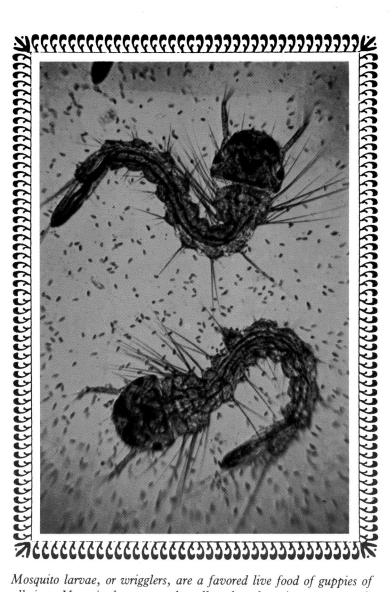

Mosquito larvae, or wrigglers, are a favored live food of guppies of all sizes. Mosquito larvae may be collected outdoors in stagnant pools of water and stored briefly, very briefly, for use as guppy food. But be sure to keep the container tightly covered or a houseful of blood-thirsty mosquitoes may be the result! It's much easier (and safer) to use the various processed mosquito larvae-based foods available. Photo by Charles O. Masters.

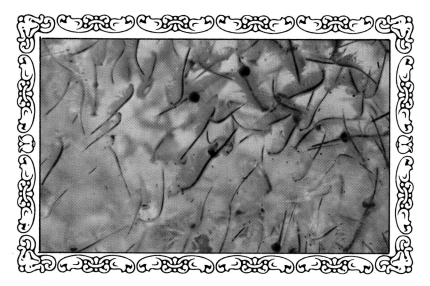

Rare are the tropical fishes that will turn their noses up at brine shrimp, and the guppy is no exception. Newly—hatched brine shrimp are a staple in the diet of young fancy guppies destined to be quality breeders. These are adult brine shrimp.

may be cultured at home. There are also other live foods, some of them found only locally and seasonally, that are nutritious. Several of the larger rotifers, such as *Hydatina senta,* the big fat *Noteus,* and the commoner *Brachionus,* are of great value, and if you are lucky enough to find a supply you can almost see the baby guppies stretch and grow before your very eyes. Rotifer cultures are often available through live food dealers advertising in *Tropical Fish Hobbyist* magazine.

Tubifex worms are a good quality live food but should not be fed exclusively to fishes, as they are very rich in protein and tend to have a "fattening" effect. Photos by Charles O. Masters.

7.
Diseases

With reasonable care the guppy is a hardy little animal and seldom gets sick. It can pick up "ich" from a bad chill or if you drop a sick fish in with him; fungus can also cause real trouble if not treated at once. The guppy

Facing page: *An early strain of the variegated fantail. New knowledge of guppy genetics and the talents of breeders working over the years have combined to produce a virtual galaxy of stunning new fancy guppy varieties.* **Above:** *These two blue delta fantails display the abnormality of Siamese twinning. Valueless as display or show specimens, they are objects of curiosity or scientific study. Photo by Stanislav Frank.*

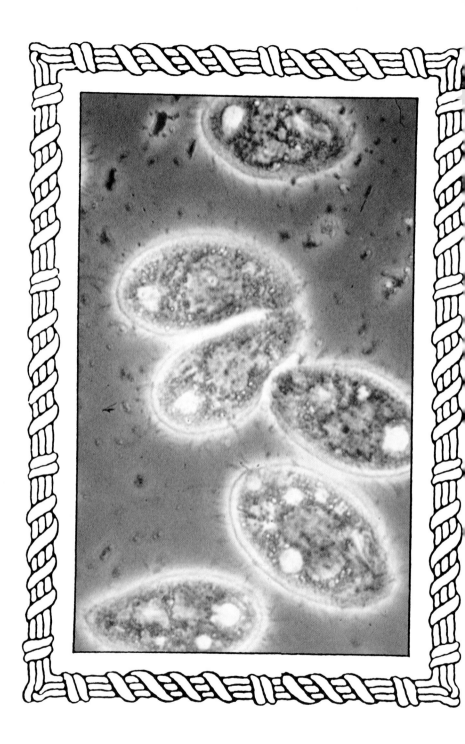

will usually respond to the good old salt treatment, which is one teaspoon of salt per gallon of water. Leave the fish in this solution for a few days or until it seems normal again. Use sea salt if possible, but always use a non-iodized salt—kosher salt is also good.

Check points

When in good health, the guppy is a perky little rascal, the males dancing around and trying to impress the females, the females moving around and feeding. If guppies sit on the bottom or hide out among the plants with their fins and tails clamped shut, they are in trouble and you had better get right at it and find out why they are uncomfortable. Check your heating arrangements. Is your filter too dirty to do a good cleaning job? Has the water become foul? Could anything have dropped into the tank? Can you see the little white spots of "ich" on fins or tail? The sooner you can correct the trouble the better chance you have of saving your fish. If they require medication, use it immediately. Don't wait around until tomorrow or next week—by then it will probably be too late.

Your pet shop people will be able to recommend medications for most common diseases. It is also wise to purchase a copy of one of the several books on fish diseases available at your pet shop.

Facing page: *An abstract painting? A photo of a squadron of UFOs? No, its simply a portrait of* Ichthyopthirius multifilis, *otherwise known as "Ich," at the swarming stage. Guppies seldom contract ich unless subjected to extremes in temperature or the introduction of a sick fish.*

8.
Summary

Here are five basic principles for raising guppies.

1) Good stock: Whatever variety you prefer, get the very best stock you can find; in this way you can benefit by previous breeding and go on from there.

Facing page: *A quintet of gold delta fantails hovers in a display tank. All of these fish show good conformation—full, well-shaped tails and dorsal fins and good color. Photo by Rudolf Zukal.* **Above:** *A blue variegated delta fantail. The true fantail is determined by the tail's being wider than it is long. Photo by Hilmar Hansen, Aquarium Berlin.*

Red variegated delta fantails. These are all males, as is usually the case when the fish are displayed in dealers' tanks, where the sexes are kept separate until sold. Photo by B. Kahl.

2) Good housing: By this I mean plenty of room; do not crowd your fish. The babies especially require a large amount of room for rapid growth and proper development. Use clean, clear water of 78°F.

3) Good food: Use a variety of foods—a high protein dry food and whatever live or frozen foods may be available in small sizes. A bit of soft algae now and then is appreciated.

4) Good care: Regular feedings in small amounts several times per day, especially for the babies. Their stomachs are small and they have to eat more often.

5) A great deal of patience and perseverance: You will be well repaid.

Suggested Reading

HOW TO RAISE SHOW GUPPIES
By Lou Wasserman
ISBN 0-87666-453-2
TFH PS-738

Contents: The Gratification Of A Guppy Hobbyist. Equipment. Water. Feeding. A Typical Day. Maintaining A Strain. Preparation For Showing. The Show Itself. History of The Modern Day Guppy. Judging Standards.
Audience: This book is intended for fish hobbyists who want to know more about the show circuit on which fancy guppies are entered into show competition and how they can raise guppies of show caliber. High school level.
Highly illustrated in both color and black and white, includes color photos of guppy varieties never before published
Soft cover 5½ x 8", 96 pages

LIVEBEARING AQUARIUM FISHES
By Manfred Brembach
ISBN 0-86622-101-8
TFH-PS-832

Contents: Which Fishes Are the Livebearers? Care of the Livebearers. Breeding Livebearing Fishes. Nutrition. How Does Live-bearing Function in Fishes? Behavior. Family Poeciliidae. Family Goodeidae. Family Exocoetidae. Family Jenynsiidae. Family Anablepidae.
Audience: For both beginners and advanced tropical fish hobbyists. Covers the rare as well as the common livebearing aquarium species for freshwater aquariums.
Hard cover, 5½ x 8", 128 pages
Lavishly illustrated with full-color photos.

ALL ABOUT GUPPIES
By Dr. Leon F. Whitney and Paul Hahnel
ISBN 0-87666-083-9
TFH PS-603

Contents: The Guppy. The Guppy's Anatomy. Physical Equipment Needed. Food For Guppies. Heredity. Practical Guppy Breeding. Guppy Disease and Ailments. Exhibiting Guppies.
Audience: This text deals with the breeding and raising of guppies. Ages 13 years and older.
Soft cover, 5½ x 8", 128 pages
42 black and white photos, 35 color photos, 25 line illustrations

GUPPY HANDBOOK
By Dr. C.W. Emmens
ISBN 0-87666-084-7
TFH PS-668

Contents: Maintenance. Water Quality. Reproduction Of Guppies. Feeding Guppies. Raising The Young. Keeping Guppies Healthy. Guppy Genetics. Selection With Minimal In-Breeding. Reversion To or Towards Type. Color Testing In The Female. Standards For Guppies. Strains Of Guppies. Prize-Winning Guppies.
Audience: Required reading for all guppy breeders. Text covers areas on measuring and adjusting salinity, saving the young, sex-limited and sex-linked inheritance. Ages 13 and above.
Soft cover, 5½ x 8", 128 pages
31 black and white photos, 63 color photos.

GAYLORD S